IN THE SHADOW OF THIS BRANCH

ROBERT PODGURSKI

DOS MADRES

2024

DOS MADRES PRESS INC.

P.O. Box 294, Loveland, Ohio 45140
www.dosmadres.com   editor@dosmadres.com

Dos Madres is dedicated to the belief that the small press is essential to the vitality of contemporary literature as a carrier of the new voice, as well as the older, sometimes forgotten voices of the past. And in an ever more virtual world, to the creation of fine books pleasing to the eye and hand.

Dos Madres is named in honor of Vera Murphy and Libbie Hughes, the "Dos Madres" whose contributions have made this press possible.

Dos Madres Press, Inc. is an Ohio Not For Profit Corporation and a 501 (c) (3) qualified public charity. Contributions are tax deductible.

Executive Editor: Robert J. Murphy

Illustration & Book Design: Elizabeth H. Murphy
www.illusionstudios.net

Typeset in Adobe Garamond Pro & Amulet
ISBN 978-1-962847-04-9
Library of Congress Control Number: 2024932181

ACKNOWLEDGEMENTS

In the *Shadow of This Branch*, *He Walks in Her Sleep*, *Decay's Worth Preserving*, and *Final Desert & Solution* have all appeared in Blazing Stadium; *In Form Filling* has appeared in SALT

Table of Contents

In my magical period I experienced strong feelings of happiness. But then a new anguish arose that was worse than the old one. I realized that in trying to express what a thing communicated, I was making a thing of the communication— an unusual and fantastic thing perhaps, but of what is not yet a thing, a matter from which things are formed.

Empty Streets
MICHAL AJVAS

A prophecy and indirection, a thought impalpable to
     breathe as air,
A chorus of dryads, fading, departing,, or hamadryads
     departing,
A murmuring, fateful, giant voice, out of the earth and sky,

Song of the Redwood-Tree
WALT WHITMAN

The mystery of dusk! Only beyond our words, where the power of our magic cannot reach, does that dark boundless element resound. Here, the word disintegrates into elements and dissolves, returns to its etymology, enters again into its depths, into its dark root. What do you mean, into its depths? We understand this literally. It is growing dark, our words are lost among obscure associations…

There are so many unborn histories. Oh, those pitiful choirs among the roots, those tales conversing with each other, those inexhaustible monologues among suddenly exploding improvisations! Is there sufficient patience to hear them out?

The Sanitorium Under the Hourglass
BRUNO SCHULZ

IN THE SHADOW OF THIS BRANCH

To Last
A living Voice with Liminal Intent

Between fading
Resonances
Wrapped and fit snug
About
       Template a form wholly evasive
Spread out even
             As it accumulates materials

The cobbler uses leather on his own

Pocsis takes on all sorts of hides
A round (en)chanter's
Call drapes over
Feelings display features'
Successive layers surface

By words and brushstrokes
Rising acts cultivate to the edge
Between objects and eyes
Where dust is always attenuating images
Light is needed to show
      In irreverence's signs

II

Working on a small engine
The smell of PB Blaster loosening
Frozen nuts and bolts whittling away
Corrosion's welds
To the mechanical mind
Makes more of lifting symmetry

And rhythm that fires
On one piston's
Single cylinder
Giving way to moving multitudes'   (errant executable
grass blades)

III

Junk trunk
Patterned dress
Toolful Intellect
With wrote song owedabout
     Fancies

Shut one out
Keep another in
For some poem's ordered dictate
     and Backside's essential
          Shades keep projecting through   a cross

More periods and epochs
Via art(i)factual obsessions
Stand out

We often beg for more
When it is already there
          In reach
                    Slight discrepancies
                    Yank the eye
                    Toward an unexplored part of the carpet
And the sound of flattened fibers rising
Up airs'
          Organically motioning arms
Makes the book about us
          Married to earth

Stand out
    Without a need
Read from the outside in
    It goes one way
Another drawn down out of aether
      Allowing for passengers
      Heading above and beyond
In place.

In The Shadow of This Branch

The canopy's fallout
      Arboreal eyes
Against I's
      And other interjections
          Separations'
              Identities

Blackened oak roots twisted about those tulip poplars'
Dis-splaying   a-mass
Writhing twisted sprawling mesh
Catching a little left-over warmth from seed shell
fragments
With something else
Not completely whisked away by gestation
Set apart (parts)
The way certain gods go
            Out
    Eglantine,
    Means
    between the extremes
        Hugs the ground
        Skirting the sky.

II

Though I saw & felt
  A feed   of the event(ual)ity
      In seeds
          That used some words
Extracted from the interior
      Heart of the backs of verbs'
              Sound mules of the trade
      Mounting semantic's labors
      Passed by actions
      Confounded intent

Cross-over br(others
by trance
Violate certain sisters of quotidian inertia
With habits in their heads

Turning with the seasons routinely
      Passed
Project these silhouettes
Are living sigils' moves
      By desire
That grows and fades
With the light of vicissitude.

Matrimonial Forest

Twigs are tongues
Say the fallen leaves' eyes
Upon how the dead wed
& Gather lives' gold
Wivestrands living imaginations
Sent thru relations
Dividing the original unity

Not quite   Adam and eve(ned) up
However in aspirations possibilities
There will always be enmwombment
In the face of the ribbing
Myth long gone awry

Enter the phantastic garden
Open to retreat
Filled with fruit first felt
Before falling on the floor
To satisfy decay's hunger
And memories
   Settled
   With growth's next cycle
Of the bio-amassed,
   All continuum's spread throughout
The great chain of being's
   Defiant measures' re-move remains.

There is so much Unknown About

Hovering, floating on unseen airs
Trodding under bush
Swimming solitary deep
Long lists and studies attest to understanding's huge gaps
Of many species

Reassuring   this epistemological defiance
                         (not to mention more)

& there is the completely obdurate crews in recognition

Life and death determinants
Arguing about our shoulders
          Dine on good & bad angels'
          Distinctions

II

The associations of a lifetime
Each person creates
A language that dies with them
We glimpse through their script
And creations

Emerging from the world's exit wound
Living is eternal as the dying that feeds it
Wording and numbering words
When they're up and we're down
They're done
But not over.

In the Fall

An entire enterprise
Dances down to earth
      By heavenly projection
      Of a tumescent star-wash welling up
      In some celestials
         The distant lights
      Come into the eyes
      Simply looking upwards and allowed
         To pour in
            Activating the crown
            Is the cup
            A catcher
            flowering interface between things
            Arrive by touching
            Power in the mind directed from reason
            Put to magics

While others dance to earth
And appear to be standing still
Steps in matter steady
Ground, the tune, of particles
      Hurdy gurdy
      Hurly Burly
    Calls upon strong measures
Trapped as catchy burdens
So many beat
         per minute
Pulverizing the melange
      To lace the nostrils'
      Blend up from the trail's bed
      A scented walkway
      Etching olfactorily

II

Some sense bleeds into another
Frame of time with its claims in mind
Instilling introspections

Sitting on a fence
A handy vantage point
On the border where trespassing is just
A state-meant of line and stewardship.

Decay's Worth Preserving

The sun grows
So,
      A thing
Imperceptibly darker
By the moment
Will
Pass by
Natal Returns
And antumbral departures'
Darkness takes a bite
from fermentation's
gentle heat
Possessing nothing
But it's a good nothing

Topping Out the Hidden Ridge

In Ken Irby's footsteps

We walked to open
                    fields
                    doing some job of it
                    about Squaw Rock and Crane's Canary Inn,
                    Chagrin Falls many years ago on your visit
                    before heading up to Gloucester for the summer
Breathed,
        To open airs
            Exchang(
-ing,
            Suspirating to our delight when you read off verse
            hands through your hair,
            reaching for the brain

                *

Travis had never seen
this new view of dense woods
Respiring back
So we made the ascent

Lines, rods of the inner
Eye for gauging concealed
cartographic "conditions hidden in nature"
Paper maps can never show

So many creative urges behind
& ahead of things
                    Wild chicory rogue growths
                    pushing up
                    through side-walk(ed
                    cracks

like little silver snake charms
rolling about in her hands
        let loose too even though from a dream
          Those serpentines are still a re-presentation and a s(talking
          effects the gait and stride from the one side to the waking
Aeration of the soil
For Ken, Gerrit, Diane, Kent,
and most recently Peteris,
          Gone to seed
          De-meated
          Demetered
          Sprung by the pullulation
               of their logoi
               always young
               the words never seam old age,
               going their own vital way
               with no other way to think of them

and the multitudes speaking out of the threshing floor
        (The older you get the more messages from the dead
         you may receive without perceiving them)
& it goes for the living
        ones as well
since death is so very relative
        —a newcomer to the group speaks
          and the rest have to figure
          out what it means
          inside
Creative ways of listening and making associations apply
when heard through and through
An insect's delicate legs scratching at the hard floor
this morning transmitting another
        , and yet another scene presenting itself
Unveiled by vantage point(ers)
Enough to drive one mad if you keep fixated on this trend

But that's ok,
       As if the meds provide any long-term relief

II

When going it alone in the mountains
       Sounds gain traction
Footfalls tuned
       To an Appalachian forest floor
Pulverizing the old leaves
       Trees live off of
         themselves
         & others' compost
         A sort of autophagous blend
         Self-cannibalization happens to humans too
         breathing and swallowing dust (and all it contains)

                They say each of us
                consumes 8 bushels
                of dead skin cells per anuum
                how much of the self
                is anyone's guess
       *

Large mica platelets alongside the trail
       Mirror reflections
       Bounced back exchange
       Literal   &fingering
       picked up some halved
       and flake off till they're just windows
       for light and form's admission
       Literally indicate that gold is nearby
       Opacities populating the gorge
       everything washes into eventually

With no one to talk to on
      top of old Bald Knob
      in the Hemlock graveyard
      Needle down
      & nothing left
      to ground
The sky just beginning to haze with ash
from Canadian fires raging this year

Bared feet felt
      their way over to the stream
      to make water
      Like a slimy eel
      Slithering over
      the earthen vibrator
      spongy wet soothing humus
before heating up again and taking on another
leg of the journey on foot.

Bells That Ring

Off Bones
Pealed
By a spectral carilloneur

Touch—the final strike
Along with a hum, some tierce
Or a few quints
In the minerals
        starring chromatics

The little chime cried
Wanting a leg
With his brother who played the spine
And sister backstroked rib cage xylophone
To a shadowy light

There's a pattern to this play
An algorithmic craving
's descent
In keys
With the lifted fabric's arising resonance
About the crowd's body
        In a basket
Rendering kennings'
bag of bones touched, tagged tones
And more pronounce the dead.

Still Able to See Through Trees

The end of Winter's lees clinging
Death
       Back
            Wash-
             ing
From the woods of Shouldn'ts
To distill a solvent grip
Always seeping out of the vegetal
Soul's silage
Fetid bed under a wintered ferment
From a mass of personae
Populating the detritus
Digesting, breaking it down
Into a richness
For the mind
       Guided
       Cyclical Growth

The self-contained entirety
Doesn't let go
Where one season intrudes upon another
Always confounding
       Creating and allowing
       Us to make non-sense by progress(ions
       Purifying with un-thought-ofs
Twisting magics,
       Like playing games
Turning round & round about all else
Where is manifesting
A nest

In the naught of roots unearthed
    Undoing dead thoughts
        Continue to speak.

(Untitled)

It's growing time
that puts eternity in motion
Planting minutes
Seeds
Gestate
Then pullulate
Hours, days, months
Years finalize the flowering
For Being
       Aionic,
              Overlord of life's
Act in words enact
Sem(e)n/tics.

Full Circle
(In the Open
        Cycles)

A phoenix bursts into flames
Feeding on ancestral seeds
Transformational diet
μεταβολη

Feet land planting

I saw space as a sieve
(actually a sleeve

Evolving
Re-volving
Vulvulational

Wraped-around a filter
A Vessel /
        κρατερ
Cup and net
For a ca(sting

All life-long's the rite
Begun at birth
In each   mark
The circle's broken

II

On one side of the mouth time exists
To make eternity pass more slowly
& on the other, more swiftly
But between them the tangle holds the helm
Purposing

III

Barely awakened by the cries of vixens (female foxes in heat)
                              Calling out at dawn
              Roaming the hills

When I was sleeping and being told to announce the wolf's back
                  Musculature, bones and all
                  After touching and marking three cardinal points
                  Its form, the mark of the beast (has four triangles in it)

IV

Seeing through
Mineral-eyes for a notion
Life as it is with bones
The Hyena's jaws have evolved to live
Off of their contents after crushing
The death of the day's selection   One
Offering—take it or leave it
Syntax of actions impacting order

Each breath's invocational baby
To touch the tongue, first
Fastened food
Something not remembered
But felt
  & understood in darkness

Raising the grains
Before going against them
With water
Exploits growing again then
Depletion's song is done for a while
Abiding by land in the body's thread
Loosened through the leaf that rests on the lap
Mouth-thing an aetheric sutra
Binding suture

In the flesh's transitional en-tranced entrapment
Holds many wrestling
  Moves, a balance woven with momentum
  Through occasion's halving open door.

For Those Dreamers

The Moon is Full
And memories
       Distinct
       Juice of an orange
       Brought up on the sun
       Making its way into the stomach
       Cellular store

Others,
       How you appear in
       Their dreams mean there
       Our pets—we're animals too
       Replace and place

     Mem – or – rise
(hanged man)
       – Or -ries
             But trees with roots
             That extend all the way
             Into every waking membrane
             Don't forget they take
                      The form of food
                      & the realization
                      Is in skin
                           Steeped

Sleep.

II

On an evening walk emerging from the woods
A full silver Lunation up on the backside
With a cast of shadows moving
Ahead of me
From all the loves I'm ever never shown
And others.

He Walks in Her Sleep

it was an endlessly floating phantom
of night on the point of dissolving into immensity,
immense in itself
Herman Broch, from *The Death of Virgil*

Of unreason
On its own
       Like a crazy cat fun-ambulating
       Or coming out of an ore collectively
       Created from the heat of unrequited lust
       So it breeds a field
          A sort of phantasy   space
       where there is a dying to come together

In its zone
       World soul   Secure
       Bridge between a moon below
       & a sun above
       plain, dark, and obscured
       Until taking full advantage of chance
       We're walking the dangerous line between them

Alchemically Honed
       Fed pain from a broken foot bone
       Alembic open through an autumn's final fall
       My third self-inflicted c(harm of 11 / 30 / 16
       Earning me a C in retrograde's movement
       Forgetting to take painkillers that evening
       And the blinding cry's juice it yielded
       A memorable drink to wash all the bitter pills away.

Like karezza sexualis (retention)
In the trance of swapna (dreaming)
Allowed to be unimpeded by inhibitions
Carried to fruition in the hidden recesses of sleep

Bound
       A confused contradiction
       Under the anchored eye
       Is a formula completing itself
       That's no lie, but the way it is

       Weren't the texts enough
       She asked perhaps herself
       What gets put in is what comes out
       Of collaborations' gone solitary
       With long letters written to a self ever stranger

Behind the mind's mouth   shut
Reason bleeds
Dry
Hells

The long haul
       Ever extracting
       The Stripped down
       Self's an extrusion
       Unwound a round between
       A halved soul
       That's had.

(Untitled)

Between sound and silence
                              Bodies at rest tend
To wear formations'
                         Compounds keep

A furrow
        Fills
                      Then runs off
A barrow
Needs bodies   in monument   to preside
                              beneath intentionally moved grounds
         Dictates   layed open
                        By desires exhumed
                        Once a dictator
                        Returned above and beyond
                        The possessing moon
                        Rings
                        Worn,
                                Heard

If inhibitions weren't stifling
Maddening cries
Would erupt into a non-stop chorus
On all the streets
A constant
Bedlamic opera staged
Yet, but not arranged
A glorious
Production for the never to be instilled
Institute: The primacy of the primal runs
Deep in veins ab-
solution.

Wand's the Will

But some are twisted and hollowed
For putting the hand in
                    Not on
          I found
                    It wraps about mine like
                    Dried gnarled fingers'
                    Weather-worn grain
                    A hole
                              Holding

Just as the ground grew
The tree that dried and left
          Skeletal remains
          Withered
          The crone
          Once gave birth to
          And nurtured
          The Young
She's ever-green
Given the cyclic
In everything's
A womb of something
Else, or
Confusion too
From always following the light

So why illumine what does well
In the dark concealments'
Cup(ping) action
Draws a variable out.

A Lifetime to Light
A Dialogue Between

Body   Soul
And rations
Of Engagements,
Sew Heads
        It is
        It ain't
        No fair
        No certifiable display

    Devotions' up First
Implication of giving one's self up
To the solitary nature of ascent,
        Assenting to the draw
        That kills off so many
        Moth-like
The closer, the brighter it is alone
And more blinding it becomes
Obviating the need for forms
That take vision over   and out

        άνεμος
Covered slowly but surely
With thought, actions, and expectations
The soul-shadow is forced
Out of its undoings
So take it or eat it else
Embodiment rules because

It is terrible, to be sure, that the incantations of the women can make the moon fall into a mirror case, or dunk it, when full, into a silver bucket with sopping stars, or fry it like a yellow jelly fish in a pan

The body's unexpected

All its reality is a realm

Thoughts compose
A wish
A dish
      Under the tables of coherency

Signals such as
The black snake halts
Facing the Heron
Squawks
As it takes flight due NW
Walking I turn away and go back.

                                             Avoiding Invading
                                             A Void is Aiding
                                           Seclusion

In solitude's generative dialectic
A revolving door on a spherical hinge
Speaker to audience—if the speaker is listening
Then out the other side may be in
Depending on how the exchange's framed
      If by purges and introspection
      The reflections mean
      & make it
      The way in-
      sight

By noise and constant stimuli
The overload overlord's
Continual smudging
We think about
Is part of the reflective screen
Glass sandwiched quicksilver

Motions they're phantasms
Sharpening details from the other
Mother's side

Where thoughts often engage and out-think themselves
Into other things
May be alive
              Wait, watch, and listen for

II

Too light?
Frivolity has its place
In measured doses
Can't be too much
of a write-off
Unless more is less
That it often becomes nowadays
By the banquet of opposites
Lies the product of our *other sex*
              Intercourse with solvents
              Leads to another and another
              Strain of polarities
              The current stain of new pronouns
              Integrate mutating genders
              Attempt to register improper
              Being's the go-noun

What it is on top of itself
And others
Expands other responses'
Possibilities

Unidentifiable objects
Fly out of *coniunctio*
              And more

Dazzle with special defects
Due to focal issues

The closer to the alien
The less
     They are
          Presumptions
In the face   of purposes
Select us.

In The One

Season's Heat
Told tale of a book
That wrote
      On the brain
         In its own
            Blood
   Invisible before
   Details appeared
     In the half-light
         Once a kaleidoscope
           In the dark
All-ways.

Living   Leaves

For Mary Catherine Kinniburgh

Each sacred character   crawls about
On its own significance   going
Letters live
    Out of the mouth, the womb,
            All sacred gates

The isolate speech   The sound of the air changes
Is always surrounded   As it circulates about seeding leaves
Framed within   Being for harvest
An other articulation   Must be winged eggs   on the verge
                                        Of manifesting

Any opposition to this way   of thinking
Doesn't eliminate the other,
Cancels it in
                Under overarching considerations'
                Tricky task   basket full of opposites
                In proportion

To being   freed
To stammer, shout, make careless mistakes
As well as the right
To a messy life
So each wonder's
            Full chaotic disarray
Alone,
        May be a cause.

Know Coming Back

There is a w(hole
Darkness reflects
In opposition to itself
The One and minus One is Zero equals Two
Rendering an infinite realm of possibilities
Crops up where something that coincides with
Becomes
   Something else
& So on
   Top
    Toppling all
    Other thoughts will
    Buckle under absence's
    Facilitating fullness
In facted fiction
   Impacted
Play populated
   Moments
   Time defying Now's

From another angle
The hole's a wheel-
    About ecstasy unbound
    Is another and an other
    Story
Whose axes' curvature's
   Spokes
Come back to the entire
Make and minutiae

Dervish whorl(d)s
Enter here and come out mutated
Exceeding any circumference's containment
& Extend the species beyond wildest dreams.

There is a Safe Tower

NOT
       In falling off
       The Bone
       The flesh stood with
As a good barbecue
    (they say in the south)
Should do
Ribs,
       Adamic tongues
       Of the first   share
       Speech for sources
               (betrothals)

With and without a firm foundation that gives
Illusion of stability

Cast from a *shot* tower
Hardened spheroid
A drop in the process
For making shells

A scream hits first
Note

Some birds circle about
Other raptors fly off
Determined to make destination
Land   Destiny.

Transition's Return

After Walpurgis night
On May Day for Lucy

A storm has passed
Soul's last
Fiery mark
On heart
Targets
      With and without
      Permission

                  A certain little girl
                  Didn't die,
                  She just ran off
                  And joined the circus

      Having a ball
      Spinning

      Spheres

Continue
For incessant play's sake.

At Hell's Diner

For Dot C.

My fav Waitress runs the cosmic counter
Her eyes don't look much
But they're feeling everywhere
From the depths of darkest
                    sockets
                plugged into light
                          currents

For an open order
Coming across
With a big tip
Into the abyss we've made
Sin(tillate.

For an Anti-Saint of the Carpathians

In memorium Agnes Saszet

Suffered no fools'
        Suffering uncritically
Anges' scapular—
                Adorned with erudition and insight
                Born with, in discretionary displays,
                        Reinforced with common sense

As well as her departure on the eve of all-reprobate,
dissolute, souls'
Day, the heretical holiday
Where choosers face a rebirth
        By grounds dis-grac'd
        & remains erased
        Be cause, they're free

Dissolved
At dawn-
ing caustic dispensations
And a dialectic of what could have been said
Between one another
Lingers with the survived by   drive-
Buyers into progressions
That care and mutual respect
Are subject to
        Not always pretty

It's good to feel the wind without
Being able to see it
And the same with soul,
                Love,
                    And bacteria

All waiting the opportunity
To infect as they will
    that makes
    The world at any moment

While walking was important to both of us
That we should meet
Unrest and contagion,
   So much mortality in the air
     (since our college days)

Perhaps you timed it
To walk right
     Out from the exit wound
     Through the crack in the worlds
     Near Halloween's harvest
Rite to the spirit
When all else has been picked
   And is gone
From the remaining characters
Ineluctably restrained

Dying in life
Is an alignment
More than that is not possible
To understand it must have limits
By bound associations
   In any language
   And she grasped many
   Listening to the prose the people spoke
   Arose a poem
So progressive,
     That's understood

Maintaining the most terrifying thing is freedom
        Absolute and unadorned
Death has a life here that progresses
through moods and proclivities
Just like everyone else
Gives and takes

Aggie,

Accused me of lacemaking   with words
They're reflections
Off the moon-mirroring
Pools gazed upon   made
In the vast night found
Translating her and everything else
That fades beyond reach
Outside
       To continue.

All Aints' Day

The beatifically disqualified
Who couldn't make the grade
De-grade
        & fall short
Of the mark, maybe
The wrong womb
Distributed their worth
Into an ill- formed sheath
Mistaken for their magnitude
     And misunderstood
Split the confines of the label
And cut their losses down
       Above hallowed grounds
       Defiled by survivals'
       Close shaves.

Requiem for the Unrequited

Loving being often
Resides behind eyes
Murdered by minutes

Taking Hold of Water

For Peteris Cedrins
11.12.1964 - 8.7.2022

By sight
Rotting wood of the chairs and deck attest to
A 4th state between fluid and vapor
An in-betweeness that's let go almost anywhere
   There's an everyman's land
    Inviting borders to let their guards down
   Where matter
        Plays ball,
A testament of incursive abilities

To sense a liquid logic
   Is a wash-
     over
Every reason to watch-
words
    Are believed
    To let loose
    Out of hand-like rules
    For freedom's sake
    Over-ridden
    And born a way

By the coveted kiss,
   So liquid,
   in liquidity
   Lick quiddities
A bedlock in saviour(ing attention
Of immortality if for a moment
   and
The dissipation of time

through the glands
of every-body's
      A living clepsydra
      Emptying from their gauge of duration
      A sign
Expressed thought traces
      Through consciousness
That is time in its potency and being

Such grasp's untenable
Except by the glass
      Krater
Also nets (according to Hermes)
In its permeability

Perhaps the cat realizes
Laser red dots
Can't be caught
But a hunt's a hunt no matter
When irresistible game's
Tossed about in the mind
Is the other half
Of the real play
Extends and disappears
      Only to reemerge
Through another phase of what started out
As nothing more than what has been
Altered by consumption all along,
Visions of thirsts' abandoned plans.

Psyche's Sentence

Repeals come in 3's
Triangulated suits
Fitted
    Stripped
        Layers of form always being applied, then removed
        For Eros never exposed but disclosed in stages

His-   Her
Story   Glory

Always seen at the open description's end
Is that what the muse wants,
                    to satisfy
Depends
Perhaps on who's asking
Answers as riddles' reeds
        Distribute an aere
        Sing a certain way depending
        On how the winnowing wind
            Is moving
                About
      Seeds
    Who's keeping count?
    Of the bitch goddess's
    Seemingly arbitrary ordeals   (open transformation field)
Left alone, unobserved they have
    Their mute magic meting
Out.

Figure 'n Folds

Beckon a new phrenology
Of crease's ley-lines
In the skins

Field enveloped   (Mouth lovingly manipulated phrases)
to be read
Or made meaning
From the top down
Under hats
       Rendering personae beneath
       The whole house walks with
       Outer-wear

As simple as an antique
Trinket attracting attention
  In a crystal cabinet,
  Trumpet shaped whistle in sterling,
  With a miniature lanyard
  & 4 silver balls
  Glinting from texture's sounds
  Moon a-tuned
  Collecting's anamnesis
    All about
       Inmost
        Form

Deep in the woods
Under cover—Grey Heron
Hunting
  The narrow creek's bed
As tall as
  I was approaching

Startled through the confines of the trees'
Branches negotiating them somehow to fly away

Back in the hood advice written in soap
A mini-van's rear window:
DO NOT OPEN DEATH INSIDE
But how are we supposed to eat
May be
      Just in case
            Things continue in the end

Come down to sacrifice
What is known
In order to see
Beyond
The world
-ills' at ease.

A Little Lower than the Angels

For Peter Lamborn Wilson

a life of disgrace would be long forgotten
if it were not for disgraceful writers

Ernst Junger

I

Going down,
In the currant of edible
Lights'
          Companions gather
That were shared
All along
Masticated in the mouth of motion
Chewed & consumed
Like the pearlescent elect
Noodles of midnight's cusp   craving
they're living
Banquets feeding off
One another continually

II

The Marriage Knot

For Chuang Tzu's true sage
Ignores reputation
But not certain ingredients:
Blasphemy, heresy and apostasy
In the recipe for sure fire acquisition

Looking at the feed
          Language upon a string
          That's led up to writing has spelled the end

In a ledger
For keeping the books
Maintains imbalance
Thamus understood
Thoth's bestowal was no gift at all
And that we'd all grow lazy by print

Still, the culprit's harnessed
And hobbled,
That's a hippopede
Rendered into a sign of infinity

∞

Squeezed out,
        Soma for the horse
Sacrificed,
        Emblem for the land and sky and stars

It's only a life
Staked out on a remote encampment
Where they're singing the song about
In a gathering disregarding time, day, and duty to
possessions
        With wild abandon's
        Joy of the share.

(Untitled)

Aging is   the unexpected body
By turns
Bestowed straight from birth
Weathering
Lifestorms' elements,
Unexpected pain or impediment
Delivered without warning
While in the biomass
Invoking
        No way
            Out until the game departs

Seductive scars as time capsules
Emotions & the sensuous continuum
Conjoin others beyond present, past, future
And other time defying definitions' now

It will change every time it has
And everything known
When understood
Slipping into the next moment's
Predication
        Supplanted by another
                And an other
                        Succession.

Sounding

The Canopy   unfolds
Limned by birds'
Little god voices
On this day of turkey buzzards,
          Crow
    Cardinals
                    & finches
Created citadels
Eyes surrounded by skin   subjects
To droning insects, crickets and cicada din
Blanketing the forest's span

Sounding sap
          Threading relays
          Corpuscular nerve ducts
          Handle the flow
Running down from growing up
These routes based on egg ways
Along solitary veins running depths
Round the silence
          Out for a read
          Getting a fix
          On targeted zones
Electrolytic mineral to a mind

Songs always adorning
The edge of the crown
in thought
As the sun sets   awareness'
Pitch drops, absorbed
In the shadows' being
Heralds under-

world tendencies
In their own element
            A filament
                Prepared
For glowing up.

Vision Aere's

Fill
In form
Between touchings
Hand held hands
Inescapably woven of wills
Become won
One over
Means of substance

Nothing's scene felt
Psyche's fiber
A hollow sounding
by air's motion whistles' happenstance
Empuzzling
For no reason's good.

Belief in Breath

's Housed as a matter
Of subsistence
Without subsidence

Sleeping mountain laurel buds,
Up welling auxins rising in early spring
Thought-free Bio-logic
Rooted, ensourced
& all that follows the pneumatic incursion's campaign
Against inanimacy, word deeds
Awash in the respiring emulsion
Form ruptures
Rise and fall
Molecular casualties about
The interchange with stochastic faith,
Motivations on the intake
            Exhalation, acts

Surrounded by sleeping cats   (active)
Dreams,
Between borders
In the flesh feeling the part
Within an invisible play
Where the curtains have their say

About discovered movements
Writhing like Hecate Artemis's girdling snakes
Of the noetic
      Intellectual membrane
Found   to the flowering One
Thing
After another.

In-Form   Filling

"it was noisy
inside me
in your arms"
                    Joel Oppenheimer
                    from: The Jane St Poem

Skeletal Kali remains
        Pearls as little solar digestions,
Fully clothed in flesh
Triangle, gate to her death (our anima
        Or more
But what to call the mutation
On a progress
        Cut of a past's murky remnants
        Mean little except in expansion
        Continually birthed of her own enwombment
                        Moss hiding a rock,
                        Crayfish & leeches lurking unseen
                        About a creek bed
        Or words inscribed
        In a partially composed letter
        Completed when the time comes
        To send
        One world to another.

Please Play Attention

Closely
Against itself

Whittle away cognitive tiers
Or loose traction   to all seriousness
Where the dour die younger and younger

With an eye on the road
& in the head
For safe keeping
The original on the s(h)elf
Mindful of how it reads
        The markers
So they don't take over completely
, Tool against rule

The hippopede's grammar and syntactic
Control of the pen
        Hobbling dancers

Around sign-post structures
A rector,
A rictor
We all fall down
Cushioned by a bed of our own
Ashes from burnt drafts
That maybe should have been saved
Become a buffer for the worried
What they were about

No,
They were warned
Writing's a bout.

Sleepless Facts Between

Strata
That words once meant
What words are doing
Out of hand right now
Picked up layers

> Terrible events contagious left
> to grow
>
> Ants in a row on a log
> spell out exit & return
> in their uniform motion
> with provisions

     Clothed all the way to the mouth
     Once venerated by Orphic robes
     But chewed off
     In this mastication's   remains a mash-up

The wandering Roma do what they please in caravan
settlements
One day and the next are never at that place or may as
well not have been
Unproven and so separate,   free.

Reading leaves
Knowing
Scatter
Things about stuff
Has meaning, plain and simple
By spilled salt
in design
A pinch pitched into an array
Suspension in the living water
Current electrolytic
Conducted waves
The muscle
Meat of the brain
Enjoys being
Thought of this way
    to stand on a bed of nails

More
      Uneven the better
Only because
            Those points that stand out are remembered
Because
      Resurgence
          Shows
Empty quiet streets
For rats
      And more rats
      Constantly access
         and Increase
            Unease
           Our dis-ease

A Means between extremes
Where the meanest gets attention
With the highest payment due

Arriving at an unsealing,
Place unsettling events
Deeper
By errant senses
Absurdly glorified
Nine holes connected by stays
      Rays
           Relays to the head harvesting
           Helmsman

However, something surfs deep delta waves
   And alleys
      Are wonderful
      The in-between avenues
      Shadows hide by night
      A pulsing birthing queen

Too terrifying to ever touch
Brooding,
          Breeding
                    In some buried hive
Along with a lost lover's love

How much is forgotten balances upon what is recalled
What here detraction steals shall there be given

Interment's calculating tables
          Provide dividends for the divisor
          minus funerary trappings
                    A tragedy vs. a statistic
                    frail memory fails
                    consigning one to the other
Death's always Centering.

The Reptile Flowers

Children

Upon rocks in the sun
With eyes
        Looking up from their death's
        Head's flowered petals
        Camouflaged wings (Lorca sung about
                    as real

Sights say one thing
Mobility another
      Fused   they spell
               Moves
               More than
Recall's sake

For the body's embodied
A group of the absolute
Expand and contract
On a point of wonder
Then back to the confines of that place
Where it all started made-up   in

A recension everyone was waiting for
But weren't counting on
Scratchings   that know more than their makers
Possessed.

Going for the Quit-Essence

> No, it's not true, I'm not a successful man, why
> would I be since I succeed anyway. The goal I don't
> achieve is the goal that benefits me, that I benefit.
>
> From: *Down with Success*, Henri Michaux

Of give up to get out
& what the early bird catches
Is of no concern,
   has some frozen in turn
Scrounging about the late laid overs
      will do just fine

Procrastination for samsara's sake
And basking in the joys of underachieving
May reflect some latent secret
     Worded will's
     Squandering time
A terrible thing not to waste
To believe feelings force each day
Gives a way.

Astral Rejection

Abort body for soul
Wasn't Plotinus' beef with the Gnostics
But obsession with the bawd body

Hence this life away from the stars
Distance
Clothed in counterfeit sheaths
One covering
Another
Layers of deception
Unable to control the emotional
Body— bears out   displayed
Trans-moral fibers
Take time to figure
Out about the personal eidolon
And take away valuable time
Seen the first time
Beyond
Times Recall--
          Equals an infinity

Same as a stone's

Throw
For a loop
Takes a shuttle-cock's load
In line.

Myth Mouth

Our star Sun makes the body earlier
Than the word
Steps out of line
Returns on the first breath when falling asleep
To climb back in
Digesting
   Makes a dream
   Come through
   The veil
Forming myths
Generate a life
Sign – Hands up
In the trance
   Hands down,
   Laying out cards
   Played or forgotten
   Are there
                 With matters'
                 Ceremonial day
                 Table set
                      & Serving.

Final Desert & Solution

I would like a toothpick
Alfred Jarry's last request

Just
Deserves
A latter portion   Periwinkle
Of some sub(consciou(s/platter   & prickly
At the *Pampered and Poisoned* Spa   Apple of Peru

Take a break   heart
Falling love answers
Unfailingly
For the pretty oh not petty
Lovers' fare
Will put one in his place
Set at the table
Or more for a banquet
With a soul full
Folded in
Upon the service
Of sense in/versions

Long is the light
, Darkness reaches even further
        Into each
Rolling, wrestling, roiling
Emanation's penetration
Out of sight
Impressed beyond repressed limits
To sense where the deposited force
Trees & leaves retain from rain
Charged by lighting,   an instant

Lode beyond longing
All
Satisfied

With a cell sealed off
In the uncomfortable
To comfort.

Tales of Failure
To Miss
Under
Stand Over

Her letters take form in

Assembled Wrecks

I had to cut off
Barb's eviscerated bumper
with a pocket knife
in order to drive it home
So that later we could
Put together the broken pieces
To make one great break back

At the under pass

Was Ferrini so crazy
to quit his factory job
with a year or so left
till full retirement,
Any longer and he may have had nothing
left to retire, however
for the likes of Stevens it posed no problem

Who's to say

Work Makes   Whatever
come   to mind
Out of ideas
latent as well as made to catch
depending on fatigue

Hypostases

or instant's authority
Such as measuring
triumphs against downfalls
is to subtract everything
so as not to allow for any other perspective
from which to view
every event's success inclusively
That flooded out ant hill in the yard
I meant to get to the rain got first
Now it's gone but not entirely
Such fine granules

Over (stood

Avoiding the truth or an inapparency
to be exposed at a later date
when more information is made available
Can turn everything on its head
Sounds like some public service
                              announcement
But it may be more private,
                              perverse
Than inclusion has any say about
Rounding out and over
An excluded middle
Upon closer inspection
That isn't defined
                              so much

Standing Around

About the prism
The light that reflects
once illumines within
and the rays that twice reflect
project a 2nd rainbow without
In between the two is

Alexander's dark band
Playing out, attuned to
an absence of color
The space between can't project light
Where it successfully won't meet the eye
Taking over and c(over
A mix, mysterious krasis as quarry
In concealment the unknown new
Synthesis' matter of interest out of death
May be the way Dorota, who first told me
about that dark screen, saw this unfold
   on the road after seeing Ben's wife
   Dyed by it

Stand by

All but the cremains (left over)
from fires' reading the body handled
I first recall Jim Lowell's,
   then both parents
   (The wind spiralled mother's upward)

Displayed

Flaming tongued
Mad moment
Danced out of the woods
Left an oily ash
 tenaciously adhering to touch

Exorcises

The more confusion
the more puzzle points
Beads' colors
that don't match
all mixed up
parathetically speaking
they all share the same space
eventually

Grown ignorant
drawing from mistakes

        The voices outside
                your head are the real danger

Gaining a stomach for it
's The challenge

To understand
not(with(standing
The moment necessarily
may only through consciousness' open embrace
Of each hold encounter
the greater the body to be   coming.

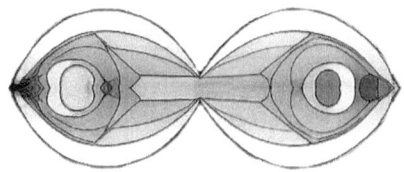

ABOUT THE AUTHOR

 ROBERT PODGURSKI has been a student of writing and the influence of magic and the occult arts in poetry for over 40 years. One result of this work is his book *The Sacred Alignments and Dark Side of Sigils,* North Atlantic Books 2019, that engages with the Enochian Angelic Magic of John Dee and Sir Edward Kelley in connection with Austin Osman Spare's theory of sigilization. The sequel, *Aetheric Alignments: Enochian Sigil Magic and the Call to the Thirty Ayres* is due in the Spring of 2025 by Inner Traditions He is also the author of *Wandering On Course*, a collection of poetry, Spuyten Duyvil Press 2014, and most recently his long-poem *Intersecting Visions Vision Intersects* was published in a limited edition by Bullhead Books, 2019

For the full Dos Madres Press catalog:
www.dosmadres.com